GRADE 3 WRITING

Fun-filled Activities

The Writing Process

Good writing starts with a plan. Here is the writing process you should follow.

Prewriting

It is important to research and make a plan before you write something.

Writing

Write out the details and ideas on a paper and read it from the beginning to the end.

Revise

Revise your first draft. Pay attention to vocabulary, text and all the details that you need to change. Edit the text. Remove text that is not needed.

Rewrite

Rewrite your draft and pay attention to the edits.

Proofread

Proofread your second draft and correct the grammar, capital letters, punctuations, spellings and organisation.

Share

Share the completed story or text.

Descriptive Writing

Descriptive writing is the description of people, places, objects, or events using appropriate details. We use a lot of adjectives to make the writing interesting.

Add a descriptive adjective to each highlighted noun to make the sentence more interesting. Rewrite your sentences.

1. The artist made a painting.

____

2. The woman baked a cake.

____

3. The boy walked through the park.

____

4. The clown made a face.

____

5. The juggler showed us tricks.

____

6. The girl looked around and found a basket.

____

7. The aeroplane sailed through the sky.

____

8. Robby's room has doors and windows.

____

The Main Idea

The main idea is most important part of a writing or story.

Supporting Details

Supporting details are facts or examples that tell us more about the main idea.

For example:

My cheeseburger looked delicious! It had crispy vegetables with freshly sliced cheese. The bun had sesame seeds and looked yummy. I couldn't wait to bite into it.

Supporting Details

crispy vegetables, freshly sliced cheese, sesame seeds

Read this paragraph. Circle the sentence that tells the main idea. Write about the supporting details.

It is raining. Polly has to go to the market. She puts on her boots and takes an umbrella. She looks out of the window. It has started raining heavily. Polly puts on her new raincoat. She also puts on her hat. Now she is ready to go to the market.

What is the main idea?

1. Polly dresses for a rainy day.
2. Polly takes a long time to dress up.

Write the supporting details.

Quick Check

Sometimes the main idea is told in the first sentence. Sometimes you need to read all of a story to know the main idea.

My Favourite Meal

With the help of these sentence starters, write a few lines about your favourite meal.

My favourite meal is.... ______

It is made with.... ______

It is my favourite because.... ______

I like to eat it when.... ______

I like to share it with.... ______

Writing Ideas And Details

Complete the following paragraph by filling in the missing information. Use the hints listed below.

________________________________(main idea). Many, many years ago, they could fly. But through the years, penguins spent more and more time in water. They did not fly much. ________________________ ______________ (supporting details). Penguins survive today because of their flippers.____________________________________(main idea). These flippers help them swim fast enough to catch food. ____________________________(supporting details)_______________. Since they have to eat so much, they usually live in areas where there are a lot of fish and squids. ____________________________________ ____ (supporting details). As a result, some penguin species are in danger of becoming extinct.

Hints

flightless bird

hatch from eggs

wings changed to flippers over time

feathers are like waterproof coat and keep them warm

use energy to swim, so they eat a lot

food taken by fishing boats

humans eat fish

not enough food for penguins because of fishing boats

Field Trip To The Zoo

Your class is taking a special field trip to the zoo. Your teacher hands you a pencil and a journal so that you can record interesting sights and sounds.

Make a writing plan of your field trip below.

Supporting details

Where are you going on a trip?

Supporting details

Who is with you? Friends? Teacher?

Main idea

Where are you going on a trip?

Supporting details

What kind of animals/creatures did you see?
Were they amazing? scary? unusual?

Supporting details

What were your activities?

Now write about your day at the zoo. Use nice, descriptive words so that your reader can imagine the animals you saw there.

Help Box

- Creepy, crawly things..
- The loud roar.....
- I don't understand why....
- What animals can teach people ....
- The cat family....

Let's Dress Up!

Write a paragraph that shares information about your wardrobe. Take help of the main ideas and the word bank to include details.

Main Ideas:

Getting dressed for a fancy dress party

Getting dressed for school

Word Bank:

hand-me-down, new, favourite, unusual, stylish, wear, fairy wings, suit, coat

Think of a moment when something very exciting happened to you. For example, winning a race or swimming for the first time.

What was your exciting moment?

Use supporting details to write a paragraph about your exciting moment below.

Use all of your senses. What did you see, smell, feel, hear and taste? These are your supporting details.

Personal Narrative

A personal narrative tells the true story of something that happened to you.

Tips to write a personal narrative

Focus on a small moment

2

Write the same way you would tell it to someone.

Start with a catchy title.

Use details to tell who, what, when, why and where.

Have a beginning, middle and end.

Describe people, places and things.

Use transition words like first, next, last.

Be careful of spellings and punctuation.

REREAD IT. Would it make sense to someone?

Use words like:

I, me, my, myself

YOU are the main character

It's about a single event.

First Day At School

How was your first day at school this year....scary, fun or exciting? Tell the story of the first part of your day.

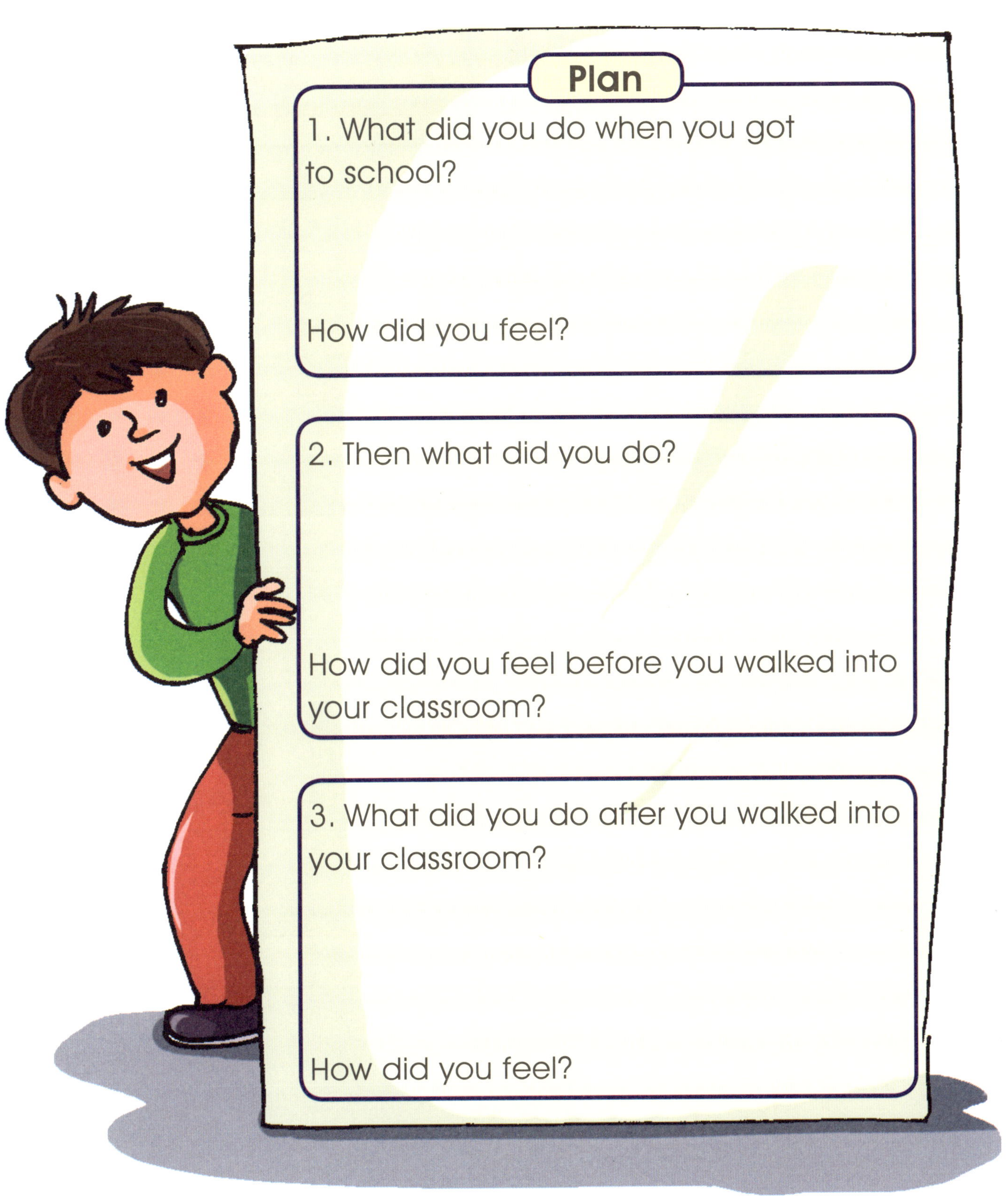

Write:

Now put all your thoughts together and narrate the story of your first day at school this year.

Learning To Ride A Bike

Fill in the organiser with information about the experience you had while learning to ride a bike.

Event :____

____

When?____

____

Where?____

____

Details______________________________

1. ____________________________
2. ____________________________
3. ____________________________
4. ____________________________

How it ended?

____

____

____

____

____

____

Write:

Now write a complete narrative on your experience of learning to ride a bike.

The Amazing Present

Write a narrative about a time you got a present that surprised you.

Write details about:

Why were you given the present?

What was it?

Why did it surprise you?

How did you feel?

Creative Writing

Creative writing is a writing in which you express your ideas and thoughts in an imaginative way. You express feelings and emotions instead of just presenting the facts.

Look at the funny scene below. Why are they running? Have they seen something? Are they running a race? What could it be? Write a paragraph describing the situation below.

Writing A Story

It is fun and exciting to write a story.
A story has:

Plot

Problem

what happens ?

Solution

Beginning Middle End

The plot of the story has a beginning, middle and end.
At the beginning of the story, you introduce the characters and the setting. In the middle, a change or conflict will happen. By the end of the story, the conflict will be resolved.

Write the name of your favourite story and fill in these details about it.

1. Characters ______
2. Setting ______
3. • Beginning ______
   • Middle ______
   • End ______

Complete The Story

Read each story beginning and complete it with your own ideas and words.

When Jack woke up, he found a lion cub sleeping on the floor next to his bed. He thought this was awesome. "Hello, lion!" he yelled. The cub, a female with a smooth coat, opened one eye and stared at him lazily. Then she turned over and fell back asleep.

Sam has been practising all year long for the big match. He has improved a lot over the season. In the first football match, he ____________________

____

____

____

____

____

____

Write Your Own Story

Make up your own story of a monster, dragon, alien or a magical creature whom you meet suddenly in your garden one day. Make sure to use the places you know in the setting.

Wacky Writing

What if you are at the salon and suddenly see a witch sitting next to you or a hair cut? Write a story about what happens next.

Writing Facts And Opinions

Read each sentence below. Write F for fact and O for opinion.

1. A farmer is someone who grows rice. ____________
2. Rice is a cereal. ____________
3. Corn tastes better than rice. ____________
4. A farmer also rears hens, cows and horses. ____________
5. A hen lays eggs. ____________
6. It is difficult to rear hens these days at farms. ____________
7. A cow has four legs. ____________
8. It takes a long time to milk cows. ____________
9. Some farmers plant apples in their orchards. ____________
10. Apples can be red, yellow or green. ____________
11. Green apples taste better than red apples. ____________
12. Farmers enjoy working in orchards. ____________
13. All crops need rain and sunshine. ____________
14. Farmers earn money by selling their crops. ____________
15. Farming is an easy task for everyone. ____________

A fact tells us something that is true and can be proven.

An opinion tells us how a person feels about something. It might tell that you like or dislike something.

Writing About Seasons

Read what John and Jane say about summer and autumn. Underline the facts.

Summer is great! It's fun to play in the sun. The days are long and warm. Children can play on the beach. August and September are the best summer months.

Autumn is better than summer. The days are cooler. Trees shed their leaves. Pumpkins turn orange. Autumn is the best time of the year.

Circle the opinion of John and Jane about summer and autumn, you agree with. Write an opinion you disagree with. Tell why you disagree. ____________________

____

____

Write facts about each season on the lines below.

Summer

____

____

____

____

____

Winter

____

____

____

____

____

Autum

____

____

____

____

____

Rainy

____

____

____

____

____

Now share your opinions on the four seasons mentioned on page 25.

Summer

Winter

Autum

Rainy

Think about some changes you would like to see in your classroom. Make it a 3-step writing. Use the help box to organise your ideas.

What would you like to see changed?

Write about the changes in detail.

What benefits would it have to make these changes?

Writing a Letter

A letter is a written message from one person to another person/ institution containing information. Letters can be friendly or formal.

When you write a letter or e-mail to a friend or grandparent, you are writing a friendly letter or e-mail. It could share family news, personal information or some other news.

Parts of a friendly letter

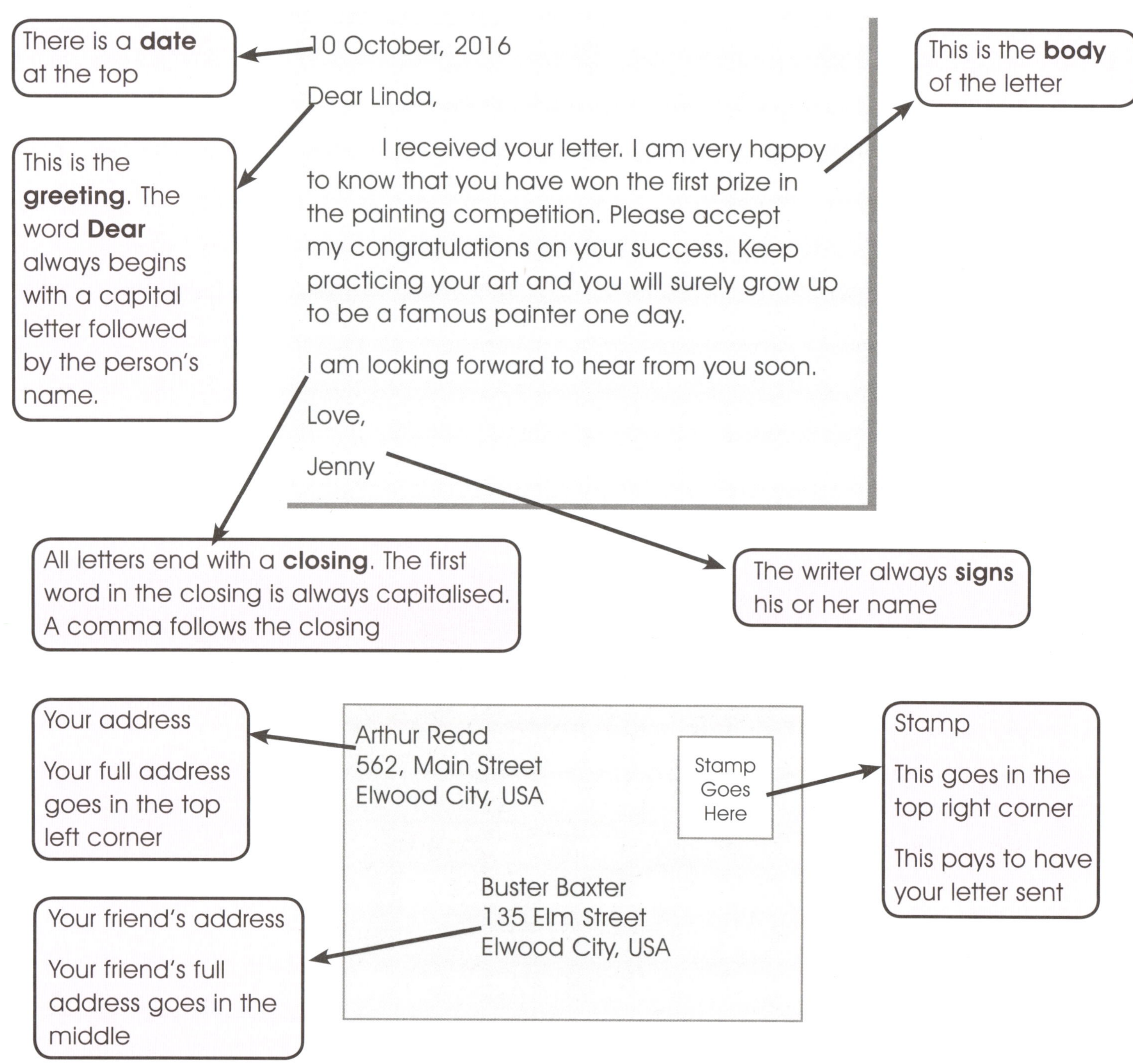

Pam wrote a letter to her cousin. Find the mistakes in the letter.

January 19 2017

Dear Cousin lily

i got your package right on my birthday thank you so much for the Big Ten dino kit. mom and i built the model of a dinasaur yesterday. Then, when dad came home. we painted it and made a big paper cap, for the dinosaur. It looks like a real dino. making these models is a fun!

Will you come visit me this summer? You should come in june It will be nice and warm. We will have fun making models of Dinosaurs together.

Love

pam

Read the letter and write a reply to James.

December 10, 2016

Dear Mac,

My classmates and I are at Camp Sunshine. There are many things to do. We made wax sculptures this morning. Yesterday, we went on a flower hunt in the nearby fields. My group won! We found all of the flowers on our list. Would you like to go to the summer camp? What would you do while you are there? Write a letter to me and tell me about the camp. I can't wait to read about it.

Love,
James

Writing A Thank You Letter

We write a thank you letter to appreciate or express thanks to someone.
Choose one writing prompt.
Using the checklist, write a thank-you letter on the lines below.

Your uncle sends you a cricket kit.	Your grandmother sends you a homemade cardigan.	Your best friend gifted you his video game.

Going On A Safari!

1. Which animal would you like to see on a safari? Write a list of 5 things you would like to know about this animal. Read books or visit a library to find more about this animal.

2. Pretend you take a safari from your hometown to Africa. Write a story about your adventure.

3. Write a paragraph about what you see and hear there.

4. Write a letter inviting your cousin to go on a safari with you. Tell him/her what exciting things you plan to do on the safari so that he is convinced to join you.

5. Imagine you are an animal that lives in Africa. Write a narrative to describe your stay at the safari.